Ernest Robert

Art of the Wild

AuthorHouse™
1663 Liberty Drive
Bloomington, IN 47403
www.authorhouse.com
Phone: 833-262-8899

Because of the dynamic nature of the Internet, any web addresses or links contained in this book may have changed
since publication and may no longer be valid. The views expressed in this work are solely those of the author and do
not necessarily reflect the views of the publisher, and the publisher hereby disclaims any responsibility for them.

Any people depicted in stock imagery provided by Getty Images are models,
and such images are being used for illustrative purposes only.
Certain stock imagery © Getty Images.

This book is printed on acid-free paper.

ISBN: 978-1-6655-6279-9 (sc)
ISBN: 978-1-6655-6281-2 (hc)
ISBN: 978-1-6655-6280-5 (e)

Print information available on the last page.

Published by AuthorHouse 06/17/2022

authorHOUSE

Art of the Wild

Crows

- Older crow siblings can help their parents raise newborn chicks
- Crows have caused blackouts in Japan
- Crows have regional defects
- Some crows can read traffic lights
- Crows fight off predators by ganging up on them
- Crows have pretty good impulse control

Peacock

- Only males have those long, beautiful feathers
- Peacock only applies to the male gender whereas females go by "peahen"
- A peacock call is not a pleasant experience for humans
- Peacock feathers are called a train
- Peacock trains (feathers) take three years to develop
- Peacock sound has a low pitch that humans are not capable of hearing

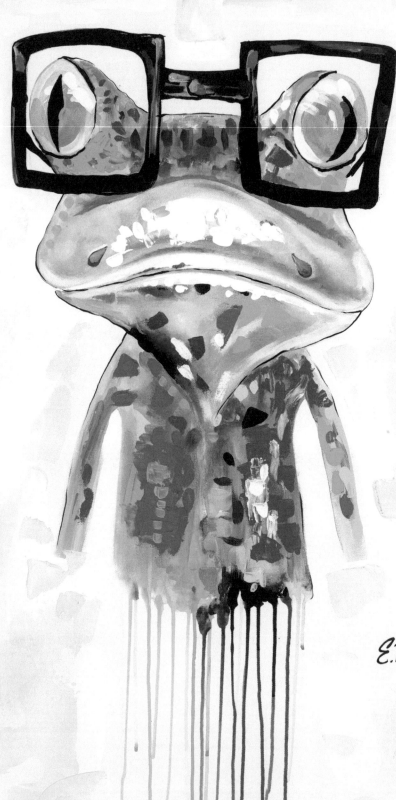

E. Robert

Frog

- There are about 4700 species of frogs
- Frogs lay their eggs in water
- Frogs are amphibians so they can breathe in water and on land
- Frogs cannot live in the sea or saltwater
- Frogs were the first land animals with vocal cords
- You can tell a male frog from a female frog by looking at its ears

Parrot

- There are around 372 different parrot species
- Parrots are one of the most intelligent bird species
- Parrots have curved beaks, strong legs, and claw feet
- Some parrots grind their own calcium supplements
- Many parrots can imitate sounds
- Parrots can live for about 80 years

Lion

- Lions are the only cats that live in groups
- Female lions are the main hunters
- Lions are big eaters
- Lions have a roar that can carry up to five miles (8km)
- Lions have amazing vision
- Lions can live twice as long in captivity

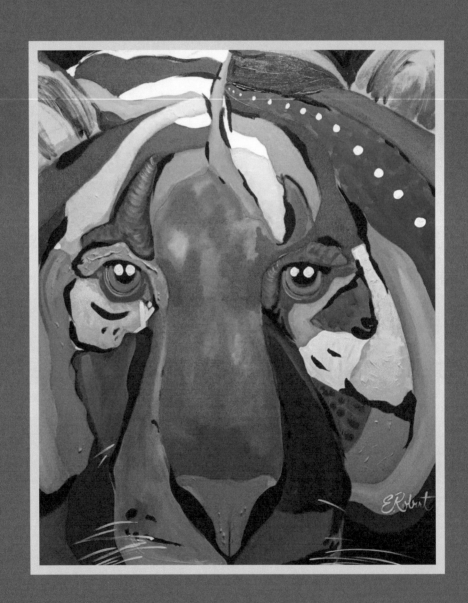

Tiger

- Tigers live about 25 years
- Tigers are the largest among other wild cats
- Tigers love to swim and play in water
- Tiger stripes are also found on the skin
- Tigers can imitate the call of other animals
- Tigers cannot purr

E.Robert

Elephant

- Elephants are the world's largest land animal
- Elephants are great swimmers
- Elephants use dirt as sunscreen
- Elephants drink up to 80 gallons of water in a single day
- Elephants are the only mammal that cannot jump
- Elephants are known to live for as long as 70 years

Rhinoceros

- Rhinos love plants and must eat a lot each day to be full
- Rhinos have small brains
- A group of rhinos is known as a herd, or a crash
- Rhinos can run 30-40 miles per hour
- Rhinos communicate by excrement
- Rhinos are the second largest mammal on the planet
- Rhinos have been around for over 50 million years

Owls

- Owls can turn their heads almost all the way around
- Owls have far sighted tubular eyes and can see prey yards aways
- Owls swallow prey whole and throw up the indigestible bits
- Owls sometimes eat other owls
- Owls are masters of camouflage
- Owls have super powered hearing

Giraffe

- Giraffes are the tallest mammal in the world
- Giraffes can stand half an hour after being born
- Giraffes can run at speeds up to 35 miles per hour
- Giraffes require over 75 pounds of food a day
- Giraffes have the same number of vertebrae as humans
- Giraffe tongues can be up to 20 inches long and are darkly colored

Shark

- Sharks do not have bones
- Sharks skin feels like sandpaper
- Sharks can go into a trance like state called tonic immobility
- Sharks have been around for 455 million years ago based on fossil scales
- Sharks are aged by counting the rings on their vertebrae
- Blue sharks are very blue

23

Panda

- Pandas have lots of teeth 42
- Pandas love bamboo they spend at least 12 hours a day eating
- Pandas do not hibernate
- Pandas have false thumbs
- Pandas can swim
- Pandas are carnivores

Cat

- Cats on average have 244 bones
- A house cat is genetically 95.6% tiger
- Cats can jump five times their height
- Cats have an extra organ that allows them to taste scents in the air
- Cat whiskers are the same width as their body
- Cats can dream

Printed in the United States
by Baker & Taylor Publisher Services